Adam and Eve

Written and Illustrated
by Gwenn Huot

To order additional copies of this book, contact:
Xlibris
844-714-8691
www.Xlibris.com
Orders@Xlibris.com

ISBN: Softcover 978-1-4363-6838-4
       EBook   978-1-6641-4910-6

Print information available on the last page

Rev. date: 12/18/2020

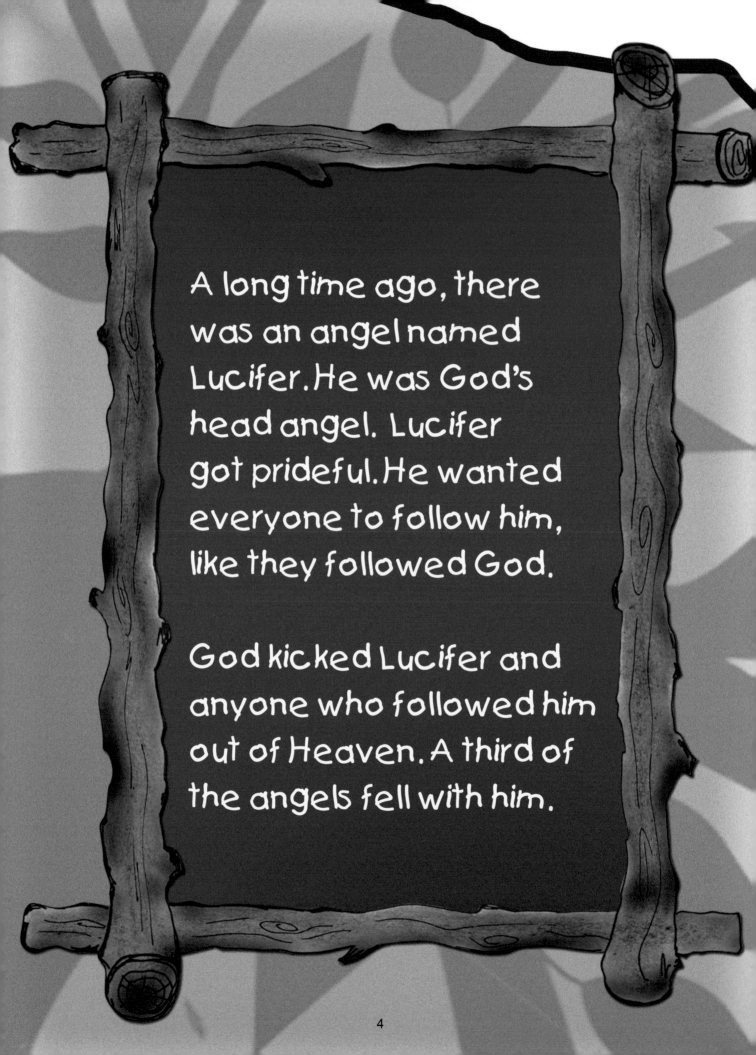

A long time ago, there was an angel named Lucifer. He was God's head angel. Lucifer got prideful. He wanted everyone to follow him, like they followed God.

God kicked Lucifer and anyone who followed him out of Heaven. A third of the angels fell with him.

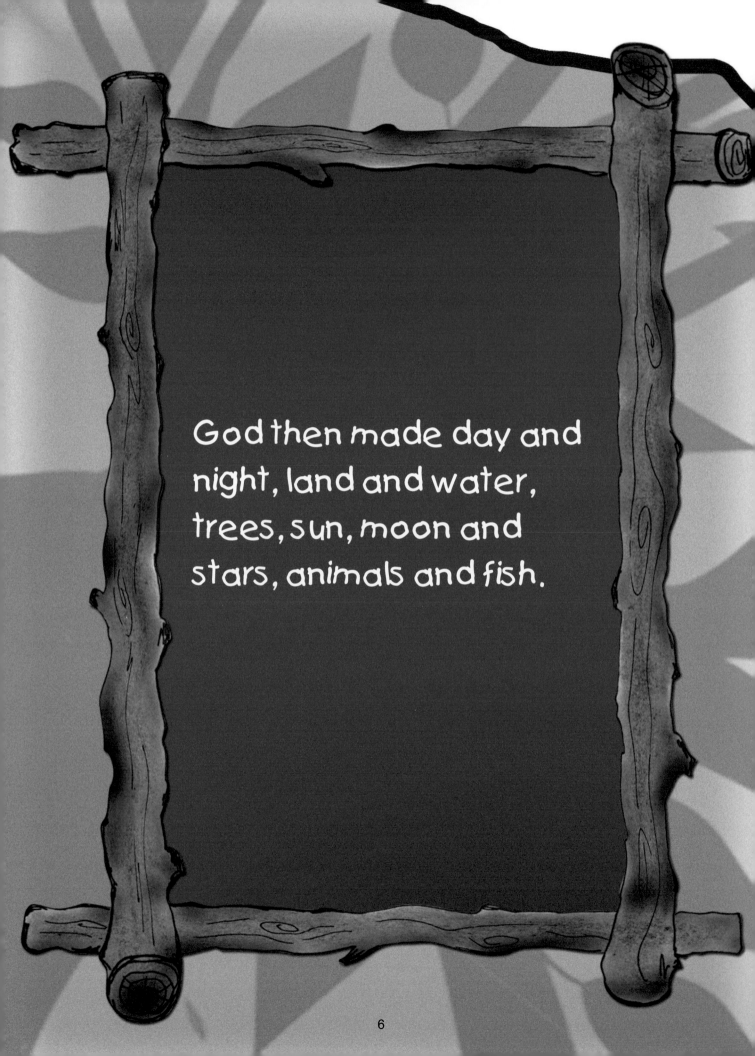

God then made day and night, land and water, trees, sun, moon and stars, animals and fish.

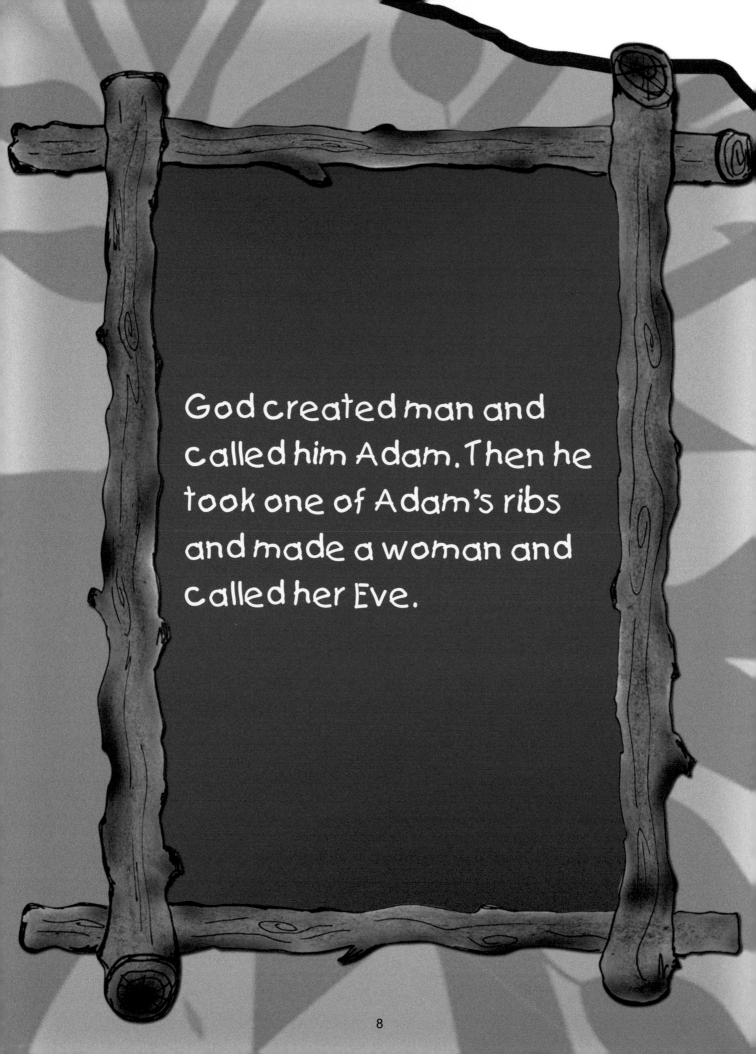

God created man and called him Adam. Then he took one of Adam's ribs and made a woman and called her Eve.

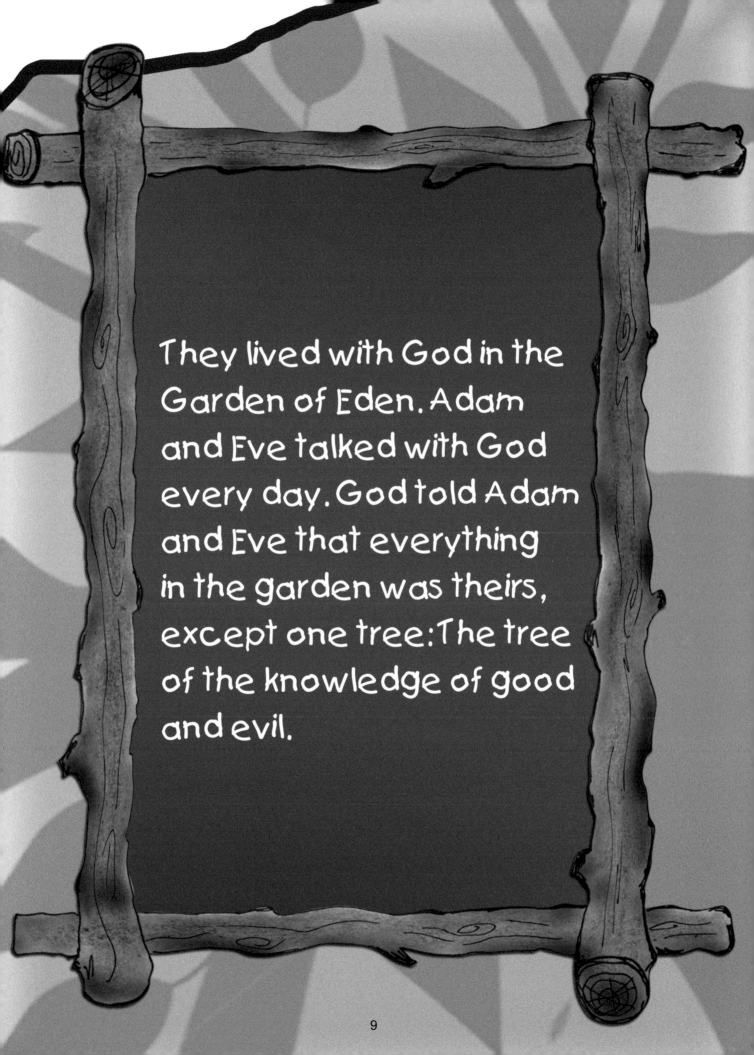

They lived with God in the Garden of Eden. Adam and Eve talked with God every day. God told Adam and Eve that everything in the garden was theirs, except one tree: The tree of the knowledge of good and evil.

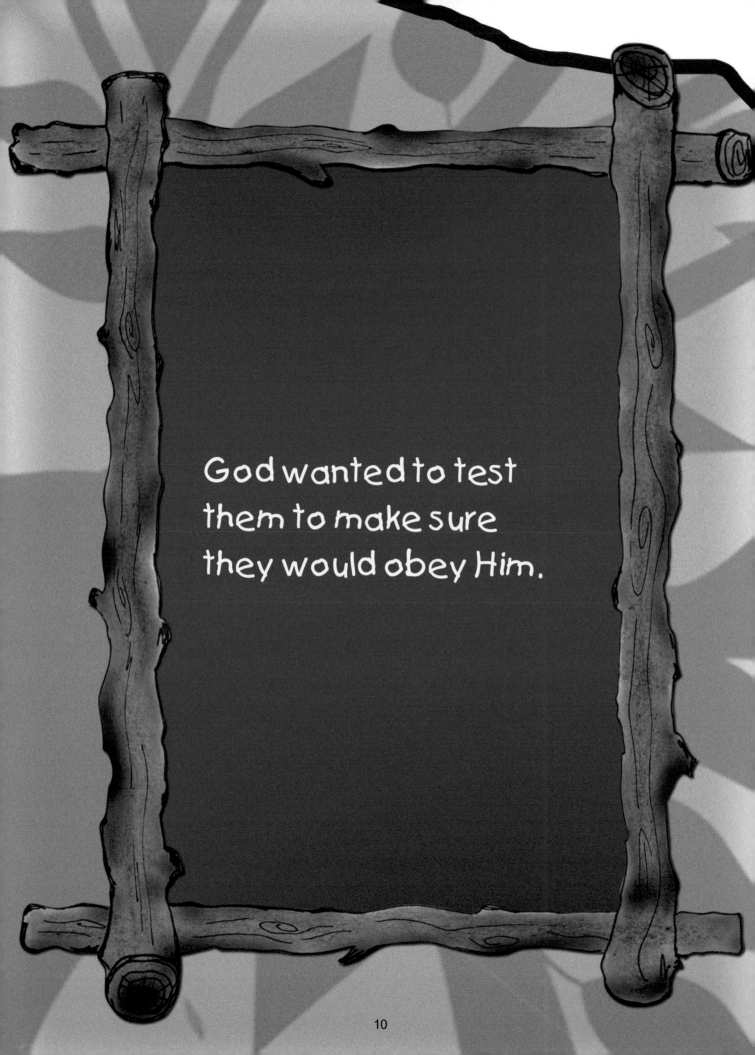

God wanted to test
them to make sure
they would obey Him.

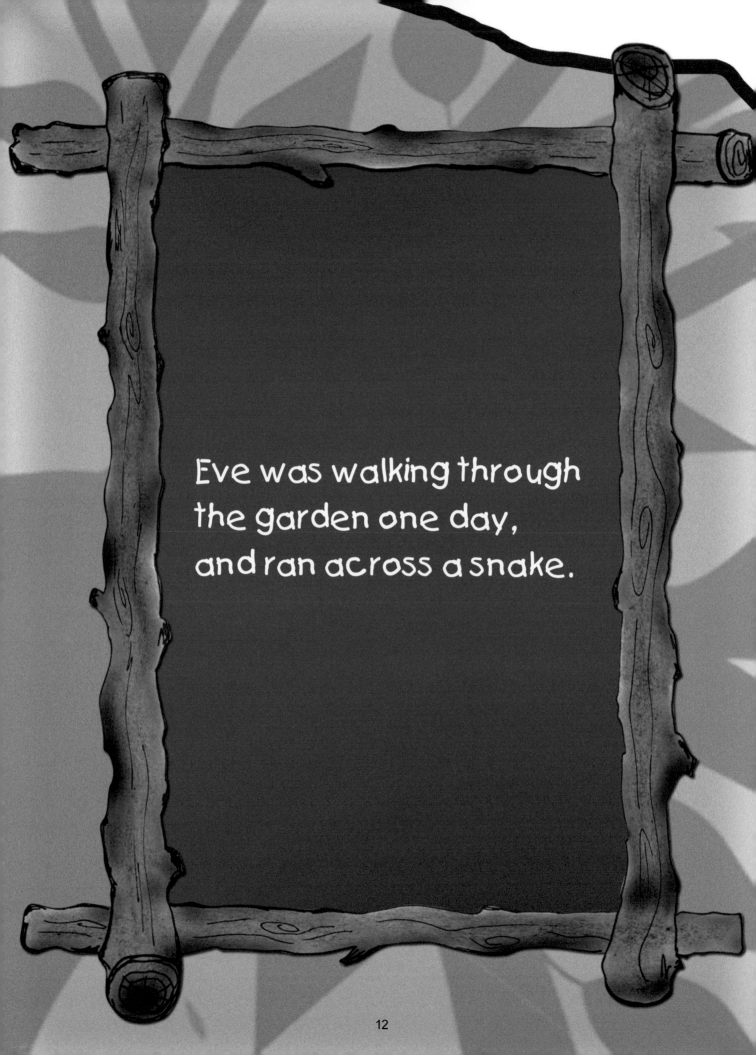

Eve was walking through the garden one day, and ran across a snake.

The snake was really Lucifer (or satan) the fallen angel. The snake lied to her and told Eve if she ate the fruit of the tree of knowledge of good and evil, she would be more powerful than God.

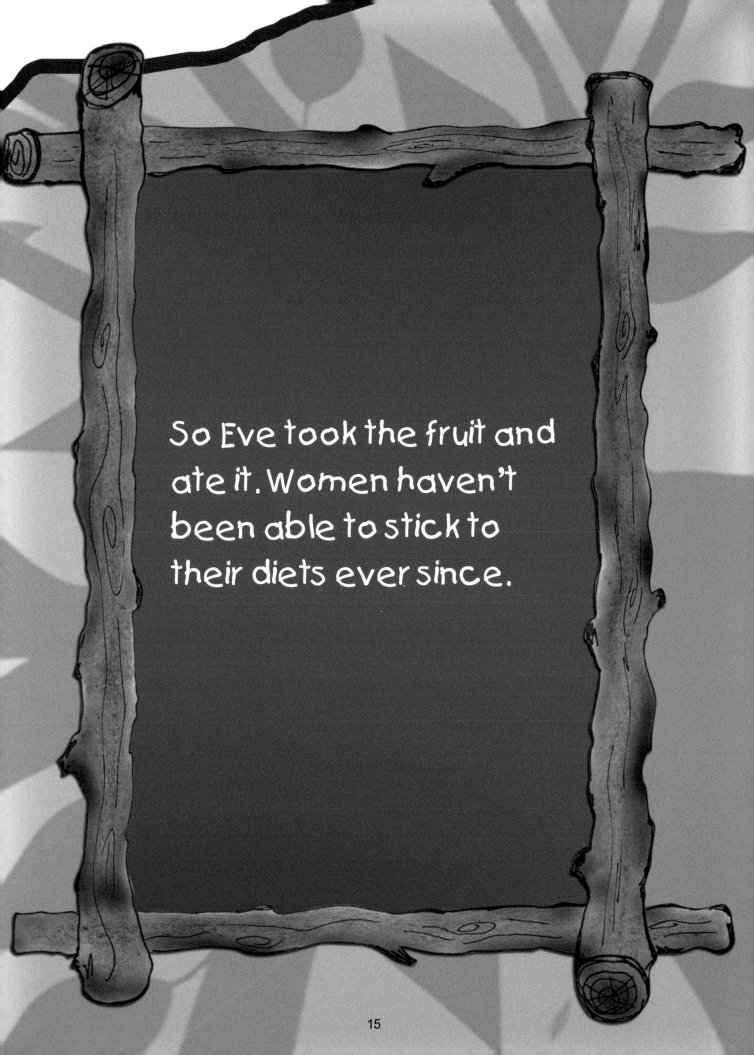

So Eve took the fruit and ate it. Women haven't been able to stick to their diets ever since.

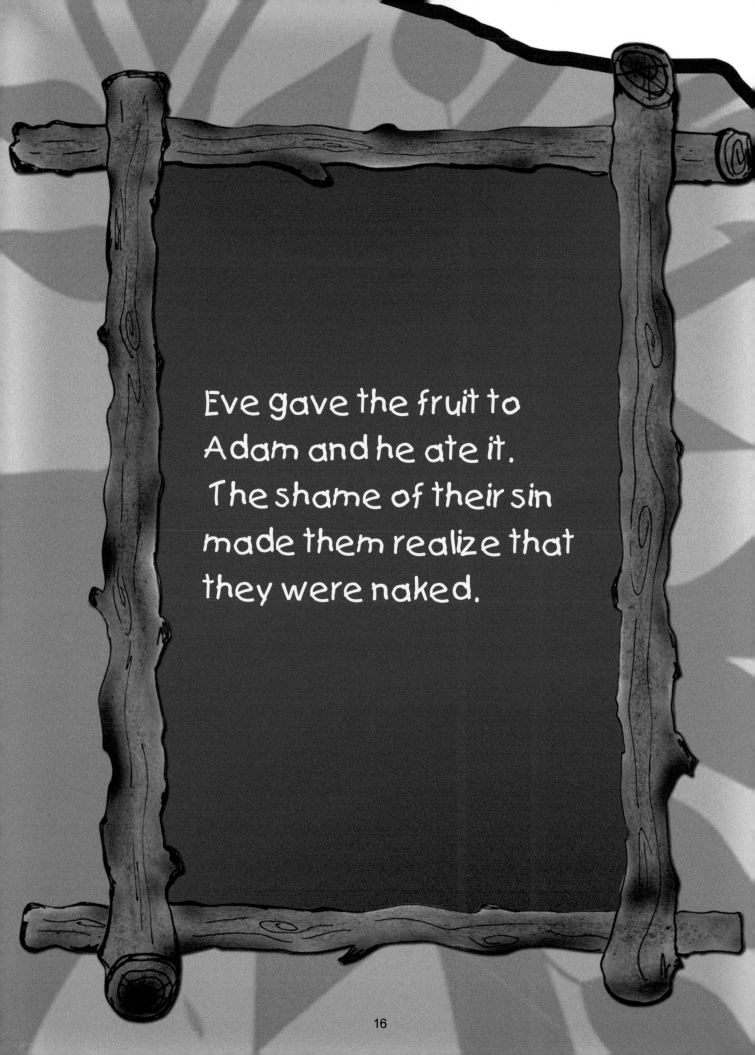

Eve gave the fruit to Adam and he ate it. The shame of their sin made them realize that they were naked.

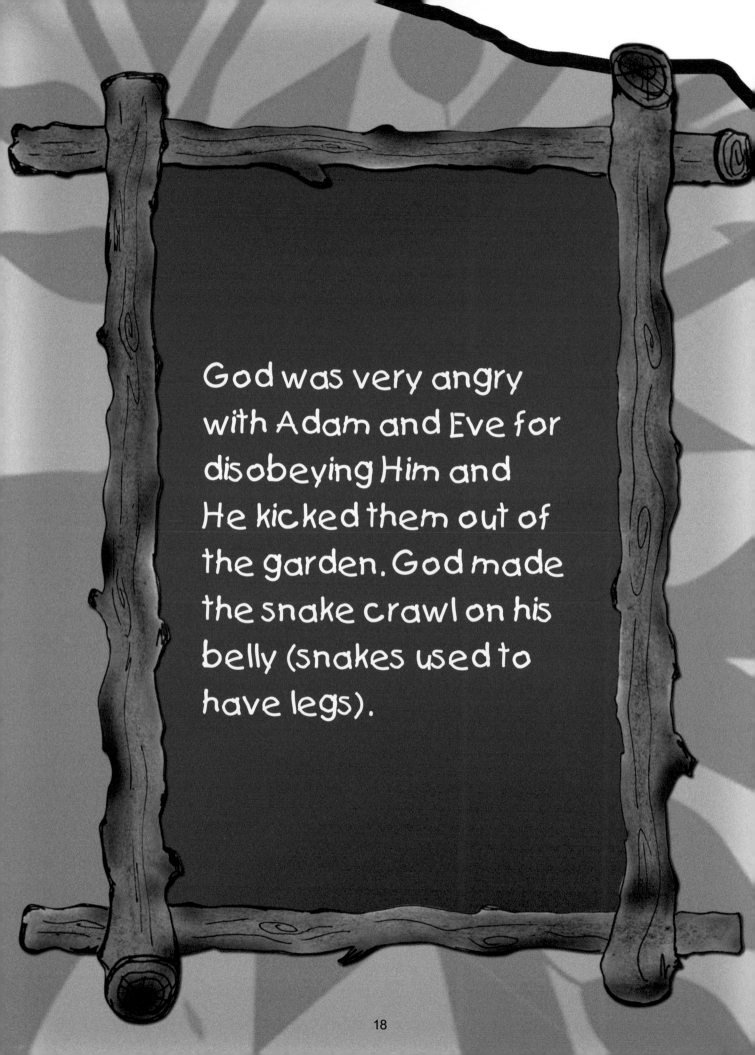

God was very angry
with Adam and Eve for
disobeying Him and
He kicked them out of
the garden. God made
the snake crawl on his
belly (snakes used to
have legs).

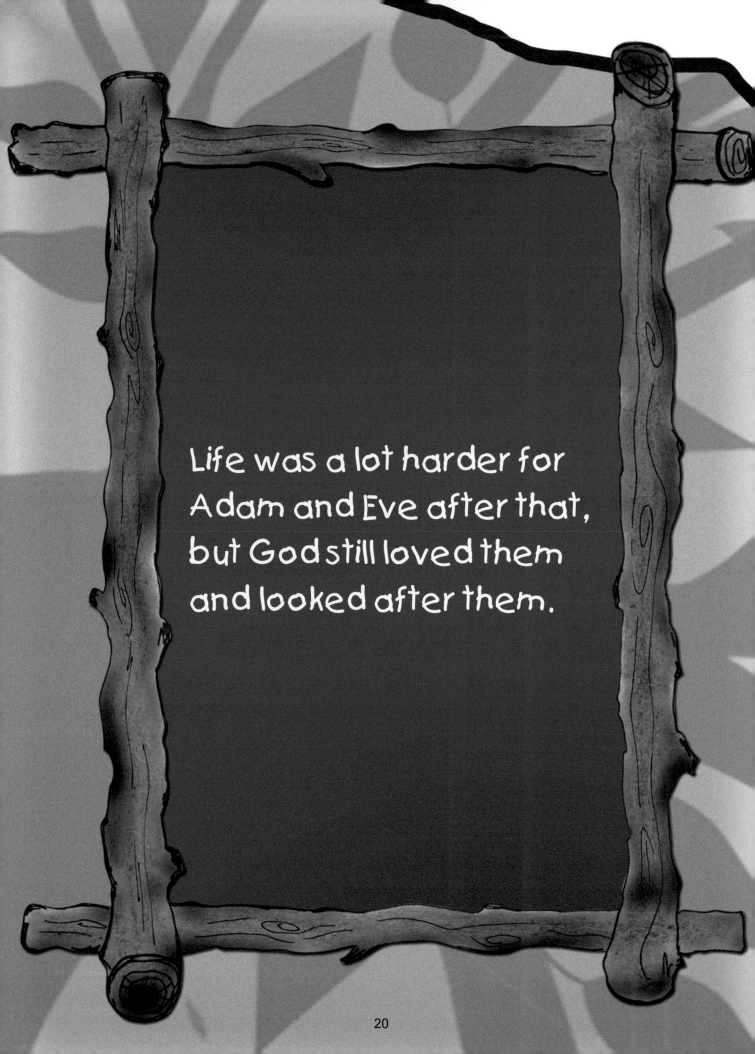

Life was a lot harder for Adam and Eve after that, but God still loved them and looked after them.

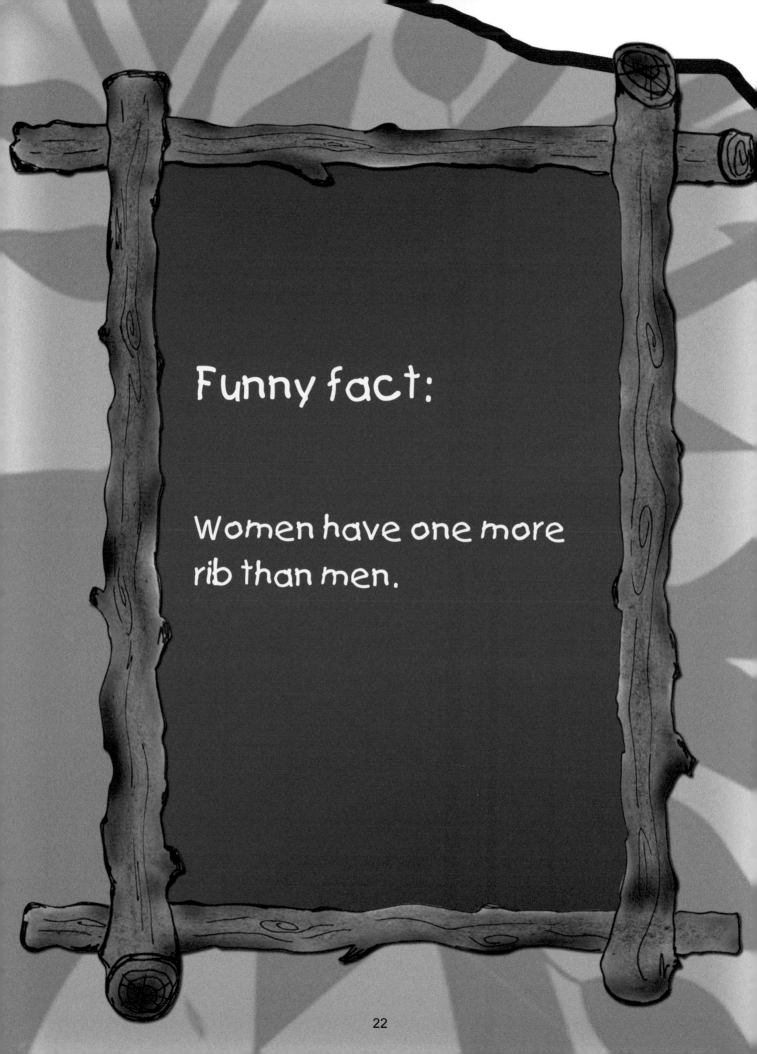

Funny fact:

Women have one more rib than men.

Printed in the United States
By Bookmasters